ISBN 978-0-243-43949-2
PIBN 10798877

English
Français
Deutsche
Italiano
Español
Português

www.forgottenbooks.com

Mythology Photography **Fiction**
Fishing Christianity **Art** Cooking
Essays Buddhism Freemasonry
Medicine **Biology** Music **Ancient
Egypt** Evolution Carpentry Physics
Dance Geology **Mathematics** Fitness
Shakespeare **Folklore** Yoga Marketing
Confidence Immortality Biographies
Poetry **Psychology** Witchcraft
Electronics Chemistry History **Law**
Accounting **Philosophy** Anthropology
Alchemy Drama Quantum Mechanics
Atheism Sexual Health **Ancient History**
Entrepreneurship Languages Sport
Paleontology Needlework Islam
Metaphysics Investment Archaeology
Parenting Statistics Criminology
Motivational

THE UNIVERSITY OF NORTH CAROLINA LIBRARY EXTENSION PUBLICATION

VOL. V   MAY, 1939   NO. 4

THE MODERN WOMAN'S BOOKSHELF

ELIZABETH CHESLEY BAITY

*Published six times a year, October, January, April, May, June, and July,
by the University of North Carolina Press. Entered as second-class
matter February 5, 1926, under the act of August 24, 1912.
Chapel Hill, N. C.*

HOW TO USE THE UNIVERSITY EXTENSION LIBRARY

The Extension Library, established to bring to the citizens of North Carolina and other states some of the advantages available to residents of the University, offers (1) study outlines based on books of special interest, and (2) the loan of these books to non-residents. To meet the growing demand for these privileges, the study outlines issued as *Library Extension Publications*, listed on the following page, and the outlines issued as *Extension Bulletins*, listed on the inside front cover page, have been prepared by members of the University faculty and others connected with the University.

TERMS FOR REGISTERING

The registration fee for the study outlines mentioned above is $7.00 in North Carolina, $10.00 elsewhere. For this fee ten copies of the program are supplied and all necessary Special References for preparing papers are loaned. The clubs are requested to submit the dates of their meetings when they register, so that the material for each date may be reserved. Sometimes it is necessary to change the consecutive order of the chapters when the demand is greater than the supply of books, but this is never done if there is a sequence of interest connecting the chapters. Cooperation on the part of the clubs in this matter is appreciated.

Additional copies of the program over ten are twenty-five cents in North Carolina, fifty cents elsewhere. The References will be sent two or three weeks in advance of each meeting and may be kept until the meeting is over. References for the less recent courses may be sent for three months or longer, and in shipments of three or four chapters. For twenty-five cents non-registered clubs or individuals may borrow material selected from the study outlines for one topic, where one or more books are required; or for fifty cents one may borrow books for an entire chapter.

TERMS FOR BORROWING BOOKS

In addition to lending books to registered clubs, arrangements may be made by which books may be borrowed for three weeks or longer by correspondence students, extension classes, teachers, pupils, superintendents, principals or general readers.

For a fee of ten cents one book may be borrowed at one time for three weeks; for twenty-five cents three books may be borrowed at one time for three weeks, provided they are not books needed for the study clubs.

Very new books not in the Extension Library collection may be borrowed through the Bull's Head Bookshop for twenty-five cents each for two weeks.

In all cases the borrower pays transportation cost both ways.

Renewal fee is ten cents per week. Overdues, five cents per day.

Always state if material is for club, school or general reading.

STUDY OUTLINES
LIBRARY EXTENSION PUBLICATIONS
VOLUME I

1. October, 1934. *The Southern Garden.* W. L. Hunt.
2. January 1935. *Adventures in Reading, Seventh Series.* C. S. Love.
3. April, 1935. *Below the Potomac.* M. N. Bond.
4. May, 1935. *Europe in Transition.* Phillips Russell & C. M. Russell.
5. June, 1935. *Other People's Lives, Fourth Series.* C. S. Love.
6. July, 1935. *The Story of Books.* R. B. Downs.

VOLUME II

1. October, 1935. *Adventures with Music and Musicians.* A. D. McCall.
2. January, 1936. *Famous Women of Yesterday and Today.* Revised Edition. C. S. Love.
3. April, 1936. *Adventures in Reading, Eighth Series.* M. N. Bond.
4. May, 1936. *Other People's Lives, Fifth Series.* C. S. Love.
5. June, 1936. *Adventures in Reading. Ninth Series.* A. B. Adams.
6. July, 1936. *Modern Plays and Playwrights.* C. M. Russell.

VOLUME III

1. October, 1936. *Adventures Around the World.* Lucile Kelling.
2. January, 1937. *The Modern Woman.* E. C. Baity.
3. April, 1937. *Literary Backgrounds of Present Day Germany.* A. E Zucker and W. P. Friederich.
4. May, 1937. *India in Revolution.* E. E. and E. E. Ericson.
5. June, 1937. *Adventures in Reading, Tenth Series.* A. B. Adams.
6. July, 1937. *The Theatre Today.* M. G. Holmes.

VOLUME IV

1. October, 1937. *Other People's Lives, Sixth Series.* C. S. Love.
2. January, 1938. *American Humor.* E. C. Downs & R. B. Downs.
3. April, 1938. *Contemporary Poetry.* Lucile Kelling.
4. May, 1938. *Building and Furnishing a Home.* E. C. Baity.
5. June, 1938. *Adventures in Reading, Eleventh Series.* A. B. Adams.
6. July, 1938. *Famous Women of Yesterday and Today.* Third Edition. C. S. Love.

VOLUME V

1. October, 1938. *Political Problems in Present-Day Europe. First Series.* Werner P. Friederich.
2. January, 1939. *Political Problems in Present-Day Europe. Second Series.* C. B. Robson, C. H. Pegg, A. B. Dugan, & J. L. Godfrey.
3. April, 1939. *Adventures in Reading, Twelfth Series.* A. B. Adams.
4. May, 1939. *The Modern Woman's Bookshelf.* E. C. Baity.
5. June, 1939. *Adventures Around the World, Second Series.* Lucile Kelling.
6. July, 1939. *At Home with the Fine Arts.* M. G. Holmes.
   Single copies, 50 cents each; in North Carolina, 25 cents.
   Advance subscription per volume, $2.00; to residents of North Carolina, $1.00. Copies sent on approval.

TABLE OF CONTENTS

INTRODUCTION

This course of study is somewhat like one of those Thursday night dishes which are a comprehensive review of the week's meals: a bit of this and a bit of that, with something spicy to warm it up. But such is the modern home-maker's reading menu, for it is her job to know a little about a variety of subjects that range from cooking, interior decorating, child psychology, economics and vocational guidance down to the personal problem of how to retain some vestige of her own individuality while spreading herself out so thin.

Women recognize today that they have a more far-reaching obligation to their families than merely to take care of their present comfort and well-being, that it is equally the home-maker's duty to try to understand the modern world and to help make her part of it a place wherein peaceful, secure human life is possible.

From the range of reading material suggested it should be possible for clubs to select programs adapted to their particular interests. Experiment with types of presentation other than the usual book review: try the duo-discussion, where two people analyze the topic; the panel discussion, where five or more take part; and the open forum period following the reviews. Occasionally ask in an out-of-the-club speaker who is especially interested in the topic with which your meeting deals.

CHAPTER I

MY COUNTRY 'TIS OF THEE

In the past we in America have thought that the quarrels of other countries were remote from our own lives. Today we know that far-away events taking place in Europe, Asia and South America, may well do more to change the course of our lives and of the lives of our children than anything that we ourselves can do. To use some of her leisure to make herself better informed about the present international issues and the current threat to democratic ideals may well be one of the most important duties the modern American woman owes her family.

The background of the present international unrest is given in the University of North Carolina Extension bulletin listed below. This study of the European situation makes it clear that the aggressor nations have certain necessities driving them which makes it improbable that our moral disapproval of their policies will have the slightest effect in checking their aggressions. In *Peaceful Change* Frederick Sherwood Dunn shows how another war could be averted if the powerful European nations really wanted peace. Meanwhile these nations prepare for war, a war which it would be difficult for the United States to escape.

Recent surveys of public opinion indicate that the people of America do not believe that the last war was worth the eight million dead, the twenty-one million wounded, and the incredible waste of resources.

We know today that the immediate change of our form of government from a democracy to a temporary dictatorship will be the first result of our entering another war; we may, if we are lucky, get back our democracy and civil rights within a reasonable period after the end of the war, but if "a state of emergency" continues to exist, or can be made to seem to, we may expect a longer period of regimentation to follow.

There are other threats to our democracy. Fascist tendencies have already been displayed by Americans of considerable financial influence. Then too there are in America certain conditions that have preceded Fascism in other countries. From *The United States, A Graphic History*, we learn that fully one-third of our people are inadequately housed, that less than 1% of our population owns more than 77% of the corporate wealth, and that the former middle class is dwindling into a class of dependent wage-earners.

Meanwhile, there is the tendency to turn more and more responsibility over to the federal government. In the Fascist countries we have examples of the extreme of this tendency: government that directs every activity of the individual, and ruthlessly sacrifices human freedom to the state. When we study the results, we are happy to live in our country, to have a press that is not solely a propaganda agent, to be able to discuss controversial matters without having to fear that one word will land us in a concentration camp. We want to continue to live in such a country. Therefore we dare not forget that if we are to keep our democracy we must use it.

SUBJECTS FOR STUDY

I. KEEPING THE PEACE

Political Problems in Present-Day Europe. by C. B. Robson, C. H. Pegg, A. B. Dugan, and J. L. Godfrey.

For discussion: Chapters II, III, V, VI, XV, and XVI. (For further study, see the bibliographies with each of these chapters.)

Peaceful Change, by Frederick Sherwood Dunn.

Discuss the peaceful solutions to international disputes that this author suggests.

Discuss the program of the Women's International League for Peace and Freedom.

II. AMERICA AND AMERICANS

The United States, A Graphic History, by Louis M. Hacker, and others.

Discuss: Agriculture surpassed by industry; class composition of American farmers; the great finance groups; freezing class relations; child labor; women in industry; national debt; the outlook for the future.

Land of the Free, by Archibald MacLeish.

Condense and read this poem. Compare the index information with the photographs.

CHAPTER II

SWEET LAND OF LIBERTY

"Liberty cannot be inherited. It must be won and won fresh for
each issue in every generation. Our father's liberties are little
help to us. The old spirit may free us but never the old words."
—From *Our Ancient Liberties*, by LEON WHIPPLE.

How well are Americans keeping the rights that our ancestors won for us? In *You Can't Do That!* there is a 47-page
list of books and articles on the topic of American civil liberties.
It is a healthy sign that so much discussion on this topic should
be possible, but it is also an indication that many people feel
that our civil liberties are far from secure.

In *You Can't Do That!* George Seldes tells something about
the tactics of the enemies of civil liberties. Among these enemies
are the professional red-baiters who see a communist menace in
the simplest restatement of the principles which Thomas Jeffer-
son wrote into our constitution. Mr. Seldes suggests that some
of these people are drawing a "Red!" herring across the path
of truth. He has also amassed certain evidence that the "Vigi-
lantes" are showing more vigilance in guarding certain vested
interests than they are in protecting the general welfare.

Mary Heaton Vorse also reports the existence of forces in
America today that are undermining the civil rights guaranteed
our people by our constitution. Her history of the C.I.O. will
make the day's newspaper headlines a little more understandable
to the reader of her book.

Granville Hicks, author of *I Like America*, was once told by
a red-baiter at the conclusion of a lecture on civil rights, "Well,
if you don't like this country, why don't you go back where you
came from!" Ultimately Mr. Hicks went back where he came
from, which happened to be the hillsides of New England where
his freedom-loving ancestors had settled three hundred years
before, and wrote this book in which he pictured our country as
it is and as it might be if we cared enough to make it so.

SUBJECTS FOR STUDY

1. VIGILANCE—AGAINST WHAT?

You Can't Do That! by George Seldes.

Discuss the author's life and his other works; display the jacket of
this book, with its quotations from the Constitution; read the definition

of Fascism and the list of organizations that have shown Fascistic tendencies.

Discuss how to break a strike; how to conduct a Red scare. Read the list of agencies that are trying to preserve American civil liberties.

Give your impression of the book.

2. AS THE C. I. O. SEES IT

Labor's New Millions, by Mary Heaton Vorse.

Tell something about the family, background, and previous work of the author.

Discuss the C.I.O., what it is, how formed, current membership. Summarize the cost of the open shop. Read the letter of the woman who set out to break the strike. Summarize chapters XI, XIV, and XV.

Review the book of the LaFollette Committee. Summarize chapter XXVII. Read (p. 289) "what it's all about."

3. A "MADE IN AMERICA" RADICAL

I Like America, by Granville Hicks.

Discuss his idea for a story; on houses; the American peasantry; the cruel choices of poverty; maintenance budgets—if you can afford them; nobody starves—much; the W.P.A. and its critics; sum up chapters VI and VII. For the figures on "the vanishing middle class" consult graphs in Hacker's *The United States*.

Summarize: Can we work together? How Fascism might appear in America; the author takes his stand; chapter X.

CHAPTER III

THE MODERN WOMAN EMERGES

"That the mentality of modern woman should be identical with
that of modern man would be not only a very strange fact, but a
very deplorable one. It is unfortunately far more nearly true
than is desirable."

—ROBERT BRIFFAULT.

Although Dr. Briffault's statement proves upon examination
to have a somewhat less than flattering conclusion, his estimate
of woman's mentality might have got him burned at the stake
a few centuries earlier. The long, long struggle for education,
suffrage, and equal opportunities for women as traced in *The
American Woman*, by Dr. Ernest Groves, should interest any
woman.

This book is the most complete study yet made of the American woman's advance in status in what is still very much a man's
world. It is the result of the author's many years as a pioneer
teacher on the subject of marriage and the family, and is the
latest of his many excellent books on these subjects.

One thing that visiting foreigners almost always comment
upon is the club-mindedness of American women. The fact that
they lunch together, meet for afternoon and evening sessions on
private and public problems, attend conventions, and, in short,
seem actually to enjoy the company of their own sex, seems
startling and unnatural to European women. For the most part,
Europeans conclude that American women have to associate with
each other because American men prefer to devote themselves to
business.

American women may admit to a germ of truth in this un-
kindly suspicion, but they feel that it is not the entire explana-
tion. Perhaps American women are less narrowly individualistic
in their outlook than women can be expected to be in countries
where wars have decreased the supply of marriageable men.
Perhaps American women are more democratic, feel more opti-
mistic about getting practical results when organized for action.

Whatever the cause, the tremendous extent of women's clubs
astonishes the reader of *Women in Two Worlds*. This study is
especially interesting for its analysis of the reasons why fed-
erated women's clubs do not have the effectiveness that they
might have.

Chinese Women Yesterday and Today will have especial interest for the women of North Carolina and Georgia because of its account of three Soong sisters, Mrs. H. H. Kung, Mrs. Sun Yat-sen and Mrs. Chiang Kai-shek. The three Soong sisters were educated at Macon, Georgia, and their father was baptized into the Southern Methodist Church in Wilmington, North Carolina, before he returned to become a leader in modern China.

SUBJECTS FOR STUDY

1. THE AMERICAN WOMAN'S BACKGROUND

The American Woman, by Ernest R. Groves.

Discuss the cultural background of the modern American woman; the effect of St. Paul's teaching; the status of women in Europe; the Colonial women; the frontier women; the women of the Civil War period.

Discuss in more detail woman's social, industrial, and educational advance; her place in the twentieth century; and the special problems that women in industry or the professions have to face. In what way is woman's status undergoing a change today?

2. HER CLUBS AND HER POLITICS

Women in Two Worlds, by Mary Ely and Eve Chappel.

The American Woman, by Ernest R. Groves.

Discuss: women win the vote; famous leaders in the fight for woman suffrage.

Discuss the fight to open colleges to women; the formation of the American Association of University Women and its history; the rise of women's social, business, and professional clubs. Name the most influential federations and clubs and tell something about their present extent and objectives.

3. SISTERS UNDER THE SKIN

The Woman's Almanac, 1938, edited by A. Donnelly and A. Archibald.

List some of the fields of work in which the American women of 1938 were engaged; name and tell briefly about some of the women distinguished in science, the professions, business, sports, social work, and in women's political and social organizations.

Chinese Women Yesterday and Today, by Florence Ayscough.

Women of the past; their girlhood, marriage, education, professions; the way of wives; the way of mothers; artists, warriors, educators.

Women of today; the three Soong sisters; Communist women. (If possible, show pictures of modern Chinese women. *Life* and *Time* have carried articles on the Soong sisters and on the Communist women leaders.)

Additional Reading:

Addams, Jane. *The Long Road of Woman's Memory*. 1916. Macmillan. $2.00.

Irwin, I. H. *Angels and Amazons.* 1933. Doubleday. $2.50.
Langdon-Davies, J. *Short History of Women.* 1927. Viking. o. p.
Lawrence, Margaret. *The School of Femininity.* 1936. Stokes. $3.50.
Mozans, H. J. *Woman in Science.* 1913. Appleton. o. p.
Schmalhausen, S. D. *Woman's Coming of Age.* 1931. Liveright. $3.75.

CHAPTER IV

WOMEN AT WORK

"Women frequently chafe against the condition that keeps them
within four walls with only children and servants to talk to
during the day and a weary, often worried man to talk to at
night. Other women who have outside interests with stimulat-
ing contacts during even a part of the day, claim that their
homes and families then are a blessed refuge for them. Some
go so far as to state that home and families, taken thus in
moderation, prove unexpectedly exciting and interesting."

—VIRGINIA COLLIER, in *Marriage and Careers.*

The problem of educating girls will never be fully solved
until someone invents a matrimoni-scope to predict whether or
not a girl will marry, what the income of her husband will be,
how much of her energy her home duties will consume, and how
long they will last. Until that time comes, the educator must
assume that every girl may need to become self-supporting either
before or after her marriage, or in lieu of it.

Just what type of education will make this possible is an
equally perplexing problem. What fields offer women the best
chance of picking up work again after the child-rearing interval?
What part-time or free-lance work could home-makers do? Such
are the problems studied by the Institute for the Coordination
of Woman's Interests and given a partial answer in the booklets
listed below.

Catherine Filene's *Careers for Women* reviews the wide field
in which women now work, and gives the advantages and dis-
advantages of each job as seen by a woman successful at it.

The great majority of the nearly eleven million job-holding
homemakers listed in the 1930 census worked in factories, in
clerical positions, or in other non-professional jobs. With most
of them it was no question of careers or of utilizing time other-
wise largely wasted, but of the necessity to make a living.

Society has begun to accept the fact that many married
women who do not have to work need for their own sakes to do
so, but society has not yet attacked the problem of providing
part-time work for women who are also homemakers. Where
there are young children needing care and guidance it is probably
only the exceptional woman who should work away from home.

Of the unquestionably exceptional women who were listed in the 1936 *Who's Who in America,* 70% of the younger group were married as against 57% of the older group. More than half of the famous women are mothers and the group average of children is 2.3. To Dr. Lillian Gilbreth, famous industrial engineer whose work has increased the efficiency of the modern kitchen, goes the palm for the largest family as well as one of the most useful careers. Her ideas on home management received a very practical turn from her experience in managing her family of eleven children.

Harry Hepner, author of *Finding Yourself in Your Work,* says that women make a distinctive contribution to industry and that, contrary to Nazi propaganda, working women in the long run create more jobs for men instead of taking work away from them.

That only the exceptional girl should leave home to seek her fortune in New York is the subtle suggestion in Munro Leaf's book, *Listen, Little Girl, Before You Come to New York.* In this book Mr. Leaf gives excellent suggestions to the job-hunting girl who, despite his advice, does go to New York. And having located the girl in the job (depending on whether she is beautiful, brainy, or just mainly "nice"), Mr. Leaf then tells her how to find a room in which to spend the few hours she can spare to sleep, how to dress up to her job, and how to eat, if that is possible on what is still left of her salary.

SUBJECTS FOR STUDY

1. FIELDS OF WORK FOR WOMEN

Careers for Women, by Catherine Filene.

Free-Lance Writing as an Occupation for Women, by Alma Louise Olson.

The Co-operative Nursery School, by Ethel Puffer Howes and Dorothea Beach.

Discuss the fields of work in which women are most successful; necessary training; range of pay; personal qualities demanded; possibility of combining work with home-making.

Discuss the coming fields of work for women; in personnel work; in vocational and recreational guidance; and in newly developed industries.

Discuss the special problem of the older woman. What existing agencies are there for training women in your state? (W.P.A., N.Y.A., Extension Work in Agriculture and Home Economics.) In what types of work are older women preferred?

Combining home-making and a job. (See chapters XVI and XVIII in Harry Walker Hepner's *Finding Yourself in Your Work.*) Discuss the advantages of a co-operative nursery school in releasing mothers for part-time work.

2. NOT JUST A JOB—BUT THE RIGHT JOB

Finding Yourself in Your Work, by Harry Walker Hepner.

The psychological approach to success in finding and keeping a job; pulling yourself together vocationally; planning to get a job; selecting the type of work by means of tests and inventories; getting along with people; turning your handicaps into assets.

3. TO ROAM—OR TO STAY AT HOME?

Listen, Little Girl, by Munro Leaf.

Explain the author's division of femininity into the beautiful, the brainy, and the nice. Mention the type of work that a big city offers to those in each of these categories.

How many of the jobs discussed are available in your community? How do living conditions for working girls compare with those offered in New York?

Additional Reading:

Hoffman, Malvina. *Heads and Tales*. 1936. Scribner. $5.00.
Knight, Mary. *On My Own*. 1938. Macmillan. $3.00.
Sullivan, Mary. *My Double Life*. 1938. Farrar. $2.50.

CHAPTER V

LIVING TOGETHER AND LIKING IT

Letter from Alabama: "Could you give me some references
that would help me write a paper on 'How to Stay Married'?"

Evidence is piling up that the topic "How to Stay Married"
is gradually nosing "Famous Ruins of Antiquity" and kindred
subjects out of their traditional place in the programs of women's
clubs. And the current crop of books and magazine articles on
"What to Do About Your Marriage" further indicates an uneasy
suspicion on the part of a great many readers that something
should be done about theirs.

This is an idea that would have seemed down-right indecent
to our immediate ancestors. It never occurred to them to con-
gratulate themselves upon staying married. You got married, if
possible, and there was very little question about your staying
that way until death did you part, which in many cases must
have been a genuine, although unadvertised, relief. Happy marriages were made in heaven. You let it go at that, and what you
made at home was more in the line of good crusty bread, succulent
pies, and endless pairs of little pants out of papa's old suits—a
state of mind for which, after all, a great deal might be said.

The authors of the books listed below give many reasons for
mal-adjusted marriages and offer certain programs for adjustment. They observe that a close connection exists between child-
hood experiences and married happiness, but they insist that
no really intelligent and earnest person need give up and take the
veil because of the imprint of the past.

Marriage clinics and marriage counsellors are increasingly
proving their value. Dr. Ernest Groves, whose book, *Marriage,*
is used as a text in college marriage courses all over the country,
believes that marriage, like any other career, pays high divi-
dends on the intelligent planning that goes into it. Dr. Hornell
Hart, in *Personality and the Family,* gives other specific suggestions for the improvement of marriage by a process of intelligent
adjustment that he calls "creative accommodation."

Many individuals who fail in their marriage relationships do
so because they are badly adjusted to life and so fail all along the
line. Some recent books devoted to the broader fields of human
relationships and of satisfaction in work will be listed in later
chapters.

Dr. Abraham Myerson, whose very interesting study, *The Nervous Housewife*, should be read by every nervous housewife who can lay her hands on it, puts one aspect of the matter pointedly when he says: "Marriage, to be successful, is based on a graceful recession of the ego in the cosmos of each of the partners. The prime difficulty is this: people do not like to recede the ego."

SUBJECTS FOR STUDY

1. THE LONG, LONG HISTORY OF MARRIAGE

Marriage, by Ernest R. Groves.
A *Short History of Woman*, by John Langdon-Davies.

Discuss the various marriage patterns that different races have evolved. How many marriage systems are current in the world today? How would you describe our own? What future forms may marriage take?

2. TURN ABOUT IS FAIR PLAY

The Man Takes a Wife, by Ira S. Wile.
The Married Woman, by Gladys H. Groves and Robert A. Ross.

The husband in theory and in practice; the father in the family circle, relations to children, to adolescents; middle age and its problems.

The wife: her chief problems and ways of meeting them; understanding herself and her reactions; adjusting to reality; summarize from these two books a working code for a wife.

3. FOR WOMEN ONLY!

A *Marriage Manual*, by Hannah and Abraham Stone.
Sex Life in Marriage, by Oliver M. Butterfield.

While the information in these books is too intimate to be used to a great extent in club discussions, conclusions can be analyzed. Circulate the books among club members who are interested.

4. MARRIAGE IS WHAT YOU MAKE OF IT

Win Him If You Want Him, by Lee Gregory.

Discuss the author's views on the following topics or read other selections of especial interest: winning him and keeping him; the money question; his ego; his work—and yours; his family; dangerous curves ahead.

Summarize the author's views on how to lose a man, and read aloud her list of things men hate about women.

Additional Reading:

Brinkley, R. C. & F. W. *What is Right with Marriage?* 1929. Appleton. $2.50.

Groves, E. R., & Brooks, L. M. *Reading in the Family.* 1934. Lippincott. $3.50.

Hamilton, C. V. T. *What is Wrong with Marriage?* 1929. Boni. $3.00.

Popenoe, Paul. *Modern Marriage.* 1925. Macmillan. $2.00.

Sanger, Margaret. *Happiness in Marriage.* 1926. Blue Ribbon. $1.00.

CHAPTER VI

HOUSEKEEPING WITHOUT HEADACHES

"The effective personality must be primarily a producer, producing more than it consumes. In other words, the effective person must acquire a predominance of skills which will be pleasing and useful to other people first, and only secondarily satisfactory to himself."

—HENRY LINK.

The dictionary may not list good cooking among the fine arts, but in almost every husband's private list it heads the ranks. Men should greet with cheers the appearance of the *Most for Your Money Cookbook*, by Cora, Rose, and Bob Brown. This little volume costs less than a pound of good steak and offers many a neat trick to those who like to eat their cake and have some of their budget money left over too. It offers specific remedies for that despondent feeling that settles down on the homemaker when she opens her refrigerator and gazes in upon two boiled potatoes, an abandoned upper-crust of roast, and some also-ran vegetables.

There are other aspects of housekeeping that are always with us. *Maidcraft*, by Lita Price and Harriet Bonnet, is a "guide for the one-maid household" that can be as heartily recommended for the no-maid one.

Sooner or later in every household as in every administration there comes the delicate question of balancing the budget. Although brides, unlike presidential candidates, are not required to have this plank in their platforms, they are usually required to come through with the accomplished fact. And with no nonsense about posterity footing the bills.

Even an old budget-maker should be able to pick up a point or two from *How to Beat the High Cost of Living*, by Ray Giles. Although you may adopt only two or three of his 865 money savers, it is interesting to see what he thinks he could do with your budget—and wouldn't you like to see him try!

SUBJECTS FOR STUDY

1. IMAGINATION WITH YOUR MENUS

Most for Your Money Cookbook, by Cora, Rose, and Bob Brown.

Give the gist of the authors' suggestions for stretching the food dollar. List the herbs that can be raised in a window-box or flowerbed; the cuts of meat not usually called for; the best buys in fruits and vegetables; and novel ideas on how to cook and eat them. Mention some unusual recipes for common foods.

2. MORE VALUE FOR LESS MONEY

How to Beat the High Cost of Living, by Ray Giles.

Read the table of contents. Compare the section on "Eat Better and Save Money" with the suggestions made by the Browns.

Discuss saving in rent; money savers for homeowners; avoiding "extras" in building; prefabricated houses; furnishing with satisfaction and economy; cutting the cost of heating.

Mention some of the unusual money-savers in keeping a car, paying insurance, and taxes.

3. HOUSEKEEPING GOES MODERN

Maidcraft, by Lita Price and Harriet Bonnet.

Read the chapter-heads to show the scope of this book. Select readings from the chapters on kitchens; the house; periodic jobs; care of children; correct service.

Explain the household bulletin board; short cuts; food values, and any other topic that seems especially valuable.

Additional Reading:

Brindze, Ruth. *How to Spend Money*. 1935. Vanguard. $2.00.

Biddle, D., & Blum, D. *The Book of Table Setting*. 1936. Doubleday. $1.00.

Cary, K. T., & Merrell, N. D. *Arranging Flowers*. 1934. Dodd. $3.50.

Farmer, F. M. *Boston Cooking School Cook Book*. 1936. Little. $2.50.

Jordan, D. F. *Managing Personal Finances*. 1936. Prentice. $3.00.

CHAPTER VII

PERPLEXED PARENTS

"Deprivation and poverty in one's personal life is the lot of those who, unaware of the wide range of possible satisfaction in the home's relationships, have not sought such personal attitudes and family activities as will realize these values."
—BENJAMIN H. ANDREWS.

The surprise of the companions of the ugly duckling when it turned into a swan is a pale and wan emotion in comparison to the shock experienced now and then by the parents of an adolescent child. It seems only yesterday that you were saying "Where did you get those eyes of blue?" and now the more pressing question is "Where on earth did you get those ideas and *why* are you behaving in such a crazy way?"

Fortunate the parents who realize—as the authors of the following books assert—that the erratic impulses of adolescents are a perfectly natural and legitimate outcome of their processes of development into an adult member of our civilization.

Margaret Mead, famous woman anthropologist, once made an interesting study of adolescents in a primitive society, *Coming of Age in Samoa.* It was her conclusion that the particular form that our civilization takes, with its restrictions upon the exploring tendencies that are a normal accompaniment of growing up, accounts in no small measure for the storm and stress of the adolescent years. Dr. Douglas A. Thom, in *Normal Youth and Its Everyday Problems,* takes the same standpoint. His book gives many case histories and should convince the land-dwelling parent of a sea-going duckling that there is no cause for undue alarm.

"What shall I tell my children about life?" is a question that has more than its full quota of pros and cons. Within one generation the tide of public opinion has shifted from Victorian repression to the other extreme of over-emphasis, and back again to the "decent reticence" advocated by the sadder and wiser post-war mother who wrote "Intrusive Parents."

This is a difficult topic for some mothers to handle objectively, and many of them still get around to it far too late to begin with the flowers and the bees, or the love-life of the oyster, whatever that may be. For these parents, *Life and Growth* is a very present help in time of trouble. The Progressive Education Association backs it, and it was written by a woman with an understanding of the questions that young people want answered and a very unusual ability to put the answers in a clear and fascinating way. Because of its stress upon the relationship between the individual and the society in which he moves, this book is equally readable for adults.

To get along successfully with "the bunch" is the strongest incentive in the life of the average adolescent. In *Ways of Work* Betty *Lyle* shows how this urge can be used to help develop good personalities and characters through the 'teen-age girls' club. The many plans and references given in this book should make it an especially valuable one to parents and teachers of young girls.

SUBJECTS FOR STUDY

1. "BUT WHY, MOTHER?"

Life and Growth, by Alice V. Keliher.

Discuss the psychology of individual differences and its value to human progress; new ways for old; the necessity for placing value on forms of work other than the professions; social sensitivity instead of fixed rules; meeting the fundamental needs of men; heredity and human progress; the social value of interest and happiness; the dependence of democracy on a recognition of the equality of human needs and the capacity of all men to change, to grow, and to become more intelligent in the conduct of their affairs.

The bibliography of this book offers an excellent course of reading not only for adolescents but for their parents.

2. "EXCUSE US, WE'RE IN OUR 'TEENS!"

Normal Youth and Its Everyday Problems, by Douglas A. Thom.

Comment on the author and his book.

Discuss adolescence and its typical physical, mental, and social problems; the adjustment to maturing sex drives; educational maladjustments; problems of conduct.

Who should go to college?

Importance of parents' attitudes; belated "getting close" to children; understanding of how parents' own needs may affect their treatment of their children.

3. GUIDING THE 'TEEN AGE GIRL

Ways of Work, by Betty Lyle.

What girls want to know; how the club can be formed; what to do; how to take care of varying interests; to help home and family relationships; health, clothing and personality studies.

Management, grouping, organization, concrete methods of arousing interest, record keeping and program evaluation; some ways that have worked; the adult adviser; her task and her rewards.

Additional Reading:

Brockman, Mary. *What is She Like?* 1936. Scribner. $1.50.

Hart, H. & E. *Personality and the Family*. 1935. Heath. $2.80.

CHAPTER VIII

YOUR CHILDREN FACE THEIR FUTURE

There are twenty million young people between the ages of sixteen and twenty-four in our country. The usual baccalaureate motto that "There's always room at the top" falls down badly before the reality of the situation. There doesn't even seem to be room at the bottom for the 40 per cent of these young people who want work and are unable to find it. As for room at the top—well, about one in a hundred can hope to find white-collar jobs. The other ninety-nine are lucky if they find jobs that offer them at least work-experience, if not a satisfying future.

The economic problem leads the field, but the 13,000 Maryland young people interviewed in Howard W. Bell's *Youth Tell Their Story* have other problems too. Their undesired leisure represents a real problem, since few communities offer wholesome recreational and social opportunities to young people who are long on time but short on cash. Meanwhile, the corner gang and the down-town dance-hall are available, cheap, and guaranteed to keep the police courts supplied with new customers.

What can parents do to help meet this difficult situation? The American Youth Commission says that the older generation must help the younger in two ways. First, public school education must face the fact that out of every 1,000 young people, only 115 will complete the first year of college. The other 885 need a lot of things worse than they need the courses that prepare them for the colleges they are never going to attend. They need vocational guidance, and an adequate vocational training that keeps up with current vocational opportunities. They need health education, and guidance in social adjustments and personal improvement. And, for society's sake as well as their own, they must have a basic understanding of the society in which they must live—how it has developed, its current actualities, and its desperate need for responsible citizens.

Secondly, communities must offer wholesome recreation to their in-school and out-of-school youth: pools, tennis-courts, community centers. How this has been done by many towns whose city fathers were just as hard-boiled about new expenditures as are your own is shown in some of the publications of the Office of Education.

It is not only the young people who are benefited by community projects in guidance and recreation. The whole community benefits by the social stimulus of co-operative planning. Juvenile delinquency records go down; the number of job placements of unemployed young people go up. Older people helping in the program find themselves with a vital new interest. Young people see themselves not as isolated units but as part of the larger social group.

I. A. R. Wylie suggests that parents cannot make good citizens out of their children by curtain talks, but only by the force of personal example and by refusing to shield them from life: "We need adult minds—young people who have grown up quickly and are mentally and morally ready to take the helm. Their task is to live from the word 'go' to a good finish. Our task is to set them quickly on the course, letting them go by living our own lives, exerting our own capacities, taking our full share of the present. Our own 'here and now' is our primary concern. The future is not. It belongs to our children. It is their 'funeral,' their party, their whatever-they-choose-to-make of it. The quicker they fit themselves for the responsibility, the more likely there is to be a future. The call to youth today is not to 'play the game,' but 'stop playing the game and get down to living'."

SUBJECTS FOR STUDY

1. WHAT ARE THE PROBLEMS OF YOUTH?

How Fare American Youth? by Homer Rainey, and others.
Youth Tell Their Story, by Howard M. Bell.

The chief problems of American youth today; the economic problem. Wanted! Schools that educate for living. Wanted! Wholesome group recreation. Wanted! Preparation for marriage.

2. ORGANIZING THE COMMUNITY SURVEY

Community Surveys, by Carl A. Jensen & H. C. Hutchins.
How Communities Can Help, by the Committee on Youth Problems.

Discuss the plan for organization that seems best suited to your community; getting under way; tie-in with local and non-local groups; membership of the co-ordinating councils.

Surveys: the starting point, framing the schedule, limiting the area, securing the workers, publicity, planning the subsequent program.

Types of surveys: education, employment, recreation, guidance. Which type is most urgently needed by the young people in your community?

CHAPTER IX

WOMEN AND PUBLIC HEALTH

Sooner or later every mother realizes that she cannot bring up her children in a vacuum. No home, however well insulated with care and money, is safe from the diseases that are allowed to rage unchecked in the poverty-stricken homes across the railroad tracks. The best guarantee for good private health is good "public health," a fairly new service that has been defined as "The art and science of preventing disease, prolonging life, and promoting physical and mental efficiency through organized community effort."

As yet the communities in America that have made this effort are too few. Paul de Kruif, America's public health reporter No. 1, again pounds home, in *The Fight for Life,* the unpleasant truths that pellagra, malaria, tuberculosis, puerperal fever which kills thousands of mothers every year, the murderous syphilis and other plagues could be prevented. The weapons to fight them have been painfully forged—all that is lacking is the public interest that will give the fighters the funds they must have.

We are fortunate in having as Surgeon General of the U. S. Public Health Service a doctor who has a long experience in public health work and a steady fury against our current practice of sitting passive while preventable plagues ravage the helpless and the innocent. In *Shadow on the Land* Dr. Parran gives a program for ridding America of its foremost plague, syphilis. If foreign forces bombed our cities we would demand immediate mobilization of the full resources of our country. Yet we ignore the enemy among us that exacts the toll of half a million new sufferers every year. This is partly because we persist in regarding syphilis as the wages of sin, writes Dr. Parran, instead of regarding it as a dangerously communicable disease fifty percent of whose victims acquire it through no fault of their own, and that could be made a rare disease for one-half the cost of one large battleship.

What can women do in this fight against disease? Dr. Parran tells us that we must make our own fight for higher standards of public health work in our own communities, working through our clubs and through local civic organizations. We must make a fight to take politics out of public health appointments, and to make possible a life career of public health work. We must give the public health service a feeling of public support, and adequate financial support to enable them to fight effectively the diseases that must be fought on a community-wide or state-wide front. Only in such ways can women help make their families safe from the "ghastly luxury" of the dreadful and preventable diseases.

SUBJECTS FOR STUDY

1. THE PEOPLE'S FIGHT FOR LIFE

The Fight for Life, by Paul de Kruif.

Discuss the fight for life's beginnings. Why is it "the people's fight?" Doctors Lee and Elliott and their contributions; the Chicago Maternity Center; its record and how it achieved it.

Read the 10-point program.

Infantile paralysis; its nature, its history, the hunt for a serum, Alabama experiment, Dramer spray. What is the future?

Tell the story of Detroit's fight against tuberculosis.

2. THE GHASTLY LUXURY

The Fight for Life, by Paul de Kruif.

How effective is the present fight against syphilis? Give this author's story of the fever machine, and its early history in Dayton; the fight of Wenger and Parran to get an adequate program.

Shadow on the Land, by Thomas Parran.

Dr. Parran and his office. Syphilis, the leading cause of death; many modes of infection; the urgent need for adequate funds for a national syphilis-control program.

The red man's revenge on the white conquerors? Columbus a probable victim; its story in sixteenth century Europe; changing attitudes towards it. American story; the case of Mr. Blank; the war program and why it was dropped; present program.

Contrast the records in Scandinavia and America as to treatment, hospital admissions, rates of incidence; show the chart on p. 111.

CHAPTER X

EVERYDAY HEALTH PROBLEMS

When Sally comes running, "Oh, mother! Bobby has stepped on a nail!" mother recognizes that here is an immediate situation that cannot be safely left to the government. But there are less obvious everyday health problems, less obvious harm that, with the best intentions, we may do ourselves and our families. These "best intentions" run up an annual bill of $200,000,000 that Americans spend for patent medicines, cold remedies, and the other fifty-nine thousand varieties of liquids and pills. What the resulting annual bill in illness and death may be, no one knows. Well, what to do about it?

First, back to Bobby and his foot. His case is amply covered in Dr. Walter Frank Cobb's *Everyday First Aid*. This book is the next best thing to having a good course in first aid. Excellent to have for emergencies, it is an interesting book to read even if you seldom witness anything more alarming than a dog-fight.

Each chapter begins with an authentic newspaper account of an accident and continues with an analysis of the situation, the first aid treatment, and the subsequent history of the patient. By this advice the reader has impressed upon him the basic principles of emergency first aid.

We may escape emergencies, but there are other problems that none of us can escape. Most of us are equipped in the conventional way with hair, teeth, and digestive systems, and most of us are continually struggling to keep this gear in running order. *Take Care of Yourself*, by Jerome Ephraim, deals with the personal care and the minor ailments of a normal person; the common cold, the too, too solid flesh, and the other common problems that would rate more serious attention were they not so usual.

Mr. Ephraim has a great deal to say about drugs and cosmetics, but Mr. Morell has written a book about them that is worth the attention of any homemaker. This author deals with the dangers of permitting the advertisement by radio of medicines and cosmetics that are not only useless but in many cases are capable of producing injuries or death.

You may feel after reading Mr. Morell's book that any woman gullible enough to pay $3.50 for a cosmetic said to bring beauty to the skin because it contains gold, probably deserves to lose both her money and her healthy skin.

SUBJECTS FOR STUDY

1. WHAT TO DO—WHEN

Everyday First Aid, by Walter Frank Cobb.

Make a list of the emergencies which every woman should know how to treat. Such a list might include first aid of wounds, poisoning, fractures, bites, highway emergencies, and illness. Discuss treatment. Summarize the main steps in any emergency. Read the list of home and automobile first-aid articles given on page 253. Compare with chapter XIV, Ephraim, and page 269 in Morell.

2. GOOD HEALTH AND GROOMING DAY BY DAY

Take Care of Yourself, by Jerome W. Ephraim.

Discuss the four essentials of skin care, selection of cosmetics, how to get a tan without a burn, the care of hair, three steps in the care of teeth.

Summarize the intelligent buyer's guide to drugs and cosmetics, Chapter I, and Chapter XVIII; your health; digestion, the common cold, vitamins, and sleep.

3. HEARING IS BELIEVING

Poisons, Potions, and Profits, by Peter Morell.

List the items on Consumer's Radio Log black-list, (p. 269). Discuss the influence of radio advertising on your family's health, (chapter VIII).

For round table discussion: pure food and drug legislation, its history and present status. Contrast the Copeland and Coffey bills, (p. 326). Which should homemakers support?

Exhibits: (1) The Black List of Cosmetics, and some current advertisements of each. (2) Products (salt, soda, chalk, soap, bay rum, oatmeal, eggwhite, witchhazel, etc.) that are equally as good as expensive beauty aids. Compare prices.

Additional Reading:

Clendening, Logan. *The Human Body*. 1927. Garden City. $1.00.
Kallett, Arthur. *Counterfeit*. 1935. Vanguard. $1.50.
Malmberg, Carl. *Diet and Die*. 1935. Hillman. $1.00.
Palmer, R. L., & Greenberg, S. G. *Facts and Frauds in Woman's Hygiene*. 1936. Vanguard. $2.00.
Palmer, B. B. *Paying Through the Teeth*. 1935. Vanguard. $2.00.
Phillips, M. C. *Skin Deep*. 1934. Garden City. $1.00.

CHAPTER XI

FIRST PERSON SINGULAR

"Charm is easy to recognize, hard to analyze, but still possible to teach to those who seem to lack it, because, like a mosaic, it is made up of many small things."
— HELEN VAN PELT WILSON.

There is practically no doubt at all that Eve's main idea in eating the apple was not so much curiosity as the desire for self improvement. This is such a characteristic human desire that a good case could be made out for its being the chief reason why *homo sapiens* (frequently known to the cynical as 'homo sap') has made his astonishing contribution to the history of the universe.

This most human of desires has been behind the success story of many a recent best-seller that lays before the reader a neat scheme for improving his appearance, his social manner, and his enjoyment of life.

The best of these books are based on the sound principle that a personality is formed in action: not by the possession of a stock of maxims and ideals, but by getting out and doing the things that we are afraid or dislike to do.

In earlier chapters we have studied the more serious jobs that offer any woman a satisfactory outlet for her spare energy and her desire to make some contribution to the world beyond the walls of her home. In this one we will relax and enjoy the typically feminine aspect of this desire for self-improvement.

Almost any woman would like to be thoroughly reconditioned by experts, to emerge as a Glamour Girl, if only for one evening. Such wishes strung end to end would reach from Main Street to Paris, and as a matter of fact do so pretty often. But most of us have to be our own experts at the job of polishing up the rather humdrum job that nature made of us.

Designing Women is a useful handbook in this program for the conservation of our natural resources. To read it is to entertain the delightful thought that we really could, if we only had time for it, learn to dress, to talk, and to act a little less like the good, trustworthy home-bodies that we are. And then we remember the sad case of Scarlett O'Hara, who was always going to be a lady as soon as she had time, but who, when time and money enough were at last hers, was so hopelessly set in her ways that it is very much to be doubted if she ever really became one.

SUBJECTS FOR STUDY

1. TRADE SECRETS OF THE SEX

Designing Women, the Art, Technique, and Cost of Being Beautiful, by Margaretta Byers and Consuelo Kamholz.

Choosing clothes; your best lines; how not to look your age; color scheming; capitalizing your face value.

Buying clothes; questionnaire before buying; clothes for occasions; how to be smart though a housewife; what is distinction in dress?

Wearing clothes; when to and when not to think about yourself; ringing new changes in on old costumes; that indefinable something.

2. "A GOOD TIME WAS HAD BY ALL"

The Art of Conversation, by Milton Wright.

Survey briefly the main points in each chapter of this book. Read your selection of the conversational exercises.

Discuss starting a conversation; good general conversation; use of repartee; thinking in dialogue; telling a story; when to argue; the cultivation of tact; saying "no" pleasantly; how to listen; the principal sins against good conversation.

3. YOU AND YOUR PUBLIC

Better Than Beauty, by Helen Valentine and Alice Thompson.

Prelude to public appearances; things to think about beforehand; why don't you ask?

You and your public; first impressions; some things to remember; how to behave; realism and charm.

Discuss "Charm can't be achieved until you recognize reality, today's situations, today's problems;" "The successful woman, at home or in business, is the woman who is contributing her efficiency and her talent as a woman;" "Make yourself over as much as is necessary to adapt your life to others, but accept yourself as you really are;" "Our true faults do not distort and spoil us. Our refusal to admit them, to accept ourselves as very inadequate human beings, is ruinous."

4. ON NOT LOOKING YOUR AGE

Look Eleven Years Younger, by Gelett Burgess.

Contrast the moods, philosophy, and mannerisms of youth with those of age. Give the author's cues for reconditioning posture, voice, costume, and manners.

Discuss marriage as a pitfall for youthfulness; the dangers that face the live-alones; the sin of negativism.

Read your own selections of Burgess-isms. A chart to illustrate many of his types of the old-young may be made by clipping pictures from advertisements.

Additional Reading:

Hawes, Elizabeth. *Fashion Is Spinach.* 1938. Random. $2.75.

Stote, Dorothy. *Making the Most of Your Looks.* 1936. Stokes. $3.00.

Story, Margaret. *Individuality and Clothes.* 1930. Funk. $3.50.

White, Wendell. *Psychology of Dealing with People.* 1936. Macmillan. $2.50.

Wolfe, W. B. A *Woman's Best Years.* 1934. Emerson. $2.25.

Wright, Milton. *Getting Along with People.* 1935. Whittlesey. $2.50.

CHAPTER XII

PURSUIT OF HAPPINESS

"Woman, will you never learn that happiness is in yourself?"
—WALT WHITMAN.

And now, after having labored so valiantly to become better citizens, we will run the risk of undoing everything by exposing ourselves to Lin Yutang's book on *The Importance of Living*.

Miss Dorothea Brande has warned all readers, including the Scandinavian, of the dangerous "rewards of failure." If *Lin Yutang* has read her globe-trotting book, *Wake Up and Live*, he gives no evidence of it. In some four hundred delightful pages he praises the rewards of failure so persuasively that Miss Brande and Mr. Pitkin will have to hasten to fill the breach lest a good many readers who have waked up and begun their lives at forty should gratefully return to rest.

In this, his seventeenth book, *Lin Yutang* writes about the enjoyment of the simple "here and now" pleasures that are possible to everyone, except to those against whom the cards are most cruelly stacked.

Dr. William Moulton Marston takes a half-way position between the two schools of thought in his book, *Try Living*. The thesis of this book is that enjoyment is not only the most essential factor in life but is also the most efficient road to a successful career. "Do what you like, like what you do!" is Dr. Moulton's formula.

Margery Wilson, whose appealing face looks out at you from advertisements of a correspondence course in charm, has written a book that deserves a less ambiguous title than *Your Personality and God*. It is interesting to observe that these three authors, the philosopher, the psychologist, and the charm specialist, agree on the philosophy that life goes on equally everywhere, and that enjoyment, and love, and work are the surest ways to solve personal problems.

SUBJECTS FOR STUDY

1. ON ENJOYING YOUR LIFE

The Importance of Living, by Lin Yutang.

Tell something about the author's life and his education; give his views on human life, on our animal heritage, on our human heritage, on luck, on the enjoyment of life, home, nature, travel, and literature.

Explain what the author means by the following quotations: "We need a certain kindness and generosity to ourselves before we learn kindness and generosity to others;" "We should be able just to look at each other and love each other without being reminded of a third party in heaven;" "Genuine literature is but a sense of wonder at the universe and at human life;" "It has seemed to me that the final test of any civilization is, what type of husbands, wives and fathers does it turn out?"

2. And Reaping the Rewards of Enjoyment

Try Living, by William Moulton Marston.

The author; how he arrived at the opinion upon which this book is built; his own profession and experiences; his views on personal happiness, on professional success, on defeat, on humor, on thinking about the past, on "They say."

Discuss: "Do what you like; like what you do, and the result is happiness, not success;" "It never pays to remain physically within reach of what they say and perform acts which they say you mustn't;" "Do not fear the future; get mad at the present;" "The world owes you nothing. But it offers you a priceless opportunity to live;" "The proof of whether you want a thing, oddly enough, is whether you get it or not."

3. Every Day Begins a New Year

Your Personality and God, by Margery Wilson.

Discuss Miss Wilson's twelve steps towards a new philosophy of living. Explain the author's reasoning in the following instances: " 'Cause' and 'effect' follow each other in orderly fashion always, not just sometimes;" "We cannot always govern what happens to us, but we can govern what we do about it;" "The solution of a problem is usually contained in the problem;" "When we are at the mercy of outside situations and personalities our pose and happiness can be snatched from under us at any minute;" "No matter where you live, or how hopeless you think your situation, keep yourself reminded that Life is everywhere at once."

Additional Reading:

Bennett, Arnold. *How to Live on 24 Hours a Day.* 1910. Doubleday. $1.00.

Brande, Dorothea. *Wake Up and Live.* 1936. Simon. $1.75.

Grebenc, Lucile. *Under Green Apple Boughs.* 1936. Doubleday. $2.00.

Hillis, Marjorie. *Live Alone and Like It.* 1936. Bobbs. $1.50.

SPECIAL REFERENCE BIBLIOGRAPHY

Ayscough, Florence	*Chinese Women.* 1937. (3)	Houghton	$3.50
Bell, H. M.	*Youth Tell Their Story.* 1938. (8)	Amer. Coun. Education	1.50
Brown, C. & R. & B.	*Most for Your Money Cook Book.* 1938. (6)	Modern Age	.50
Burgess, Gelett	*Look Eleven Years Younger.* 1937. (11)	Simon	1.96
Butterfield, O. M.	*Sex Life in Marriage.* 1937. (5)	Emerson	2.00
Byers, M. and Kamholz, C.	*Designing Women.* 1938. (11)	Simon	2.50
Cobb, W. F.	*Everyday First Aid.* 1937. (10)	Appleton	1.50
Committee on Youth Problems	*Youth: How Communities Can Help.* 1936. (8)	Gov't. Printing Office	
De Kruif, Paul	*Fight for Life.* 1938. (9)	Harcourt	3.00
Donnelly, A. and Archibald, A.	*Woman's Almanac.* 1938. (4)	Oquaga Press	1.00
Ely, M. L. and Chappell, E.	*Women in Two Worlds.* 1938. (3)	Amer. Ass'n. for Adult Ed.	1.25
Ephraim, J. W.	*Take Care of Yourself.* 1937. (10)	Simon	2.00
Filene, Catherine	*Careers for Women.* 1934. (4)	Houghton	3.00
Giles, Ray	*How to Beat the High Cost of Living.* 1937. (6)	Simon	.98
Gregory, Lee	*Win Him If You Want Him.* 1937. (5)	Hillman	1.50
Groves, E. R.	*The American Woman.* 1937. (3)	Greenberg	3.00
Groves, E. R.	*Marriage.* 1933. (5)	Holt	4.00
Groves, G. H. and Ross, R. A.	*The Married Woman.* 1936. (5)	Greenberg	2.50
Hacker, L. M.	*The United States.* 1937. (1)	Modern Age	.75
Hepner, H. W.	*Finding Yourself in Your Work.* 1937. (4)	Appleton	2.75
Hicks, Granville	*I Like America.* 1938. (2)	Modern Age	.50
Howes, E. P. and Beach, D.	*The Co-operative Nursery School.* 1928. (4)	Smith College	.75
Jensen, C. A. and Hutchins, H. C.	*Youth: Community Surveys.* 1936. (8)	Gov't. Printing Office	.15
Keliher, A. V.	*Life and Growth.* 1938. (7)	Appleton	1.20
Langdon-Davies, J.	*Short History of Woman.* 1927. (5)	Viking	o.p.
Leaf, Munro	*Listen, Little Girl.* 1938. (4)	Stokes	1.50
Lin Yu-tang	*The Importance of Living.* 1938. (12)	Reynal	3.00
Lyle, Betty	*Ways of Work.* 1938. (7)	Woman's Press	1.00
MacLeish, Archibald	*Land of the Free.* 1938. (1)	Harcourt	3.00
Marston, W. M.	*Try Living.* 1937. (12)	Crowell	1.75
Morell, Peter	*Poisons, Potions, and Profits.* 1937. (10)	Knight	2.00
Olson, A. L.	*Free-Lance Writing as an Occupation for Women.* 1927. (4)	Smith College	.50
Parran, Thomas	*Shadow on the Land.* 1937. (9)	Reynal	2.50

Price, Lita and Bonnet, Harriet	*Maidcraft.* 1937. (6)	Bobbs	1.50
Rainey, H. P.	*How Fare American Youth?* 1937. (8)	Appleton	1.50
Seldes, George	*You Can't Do That.* 1938. (2)	Modern Age	.50
Stone, H. & A.	*A Marriage Manual.* 1935. (5)	Simon	2.50
Thom, D. A.	*Normal Youth.* 1932. (7)	Appleton	2.50
Valentine, H. and Thompson, A.	*Better than Beauty.* 1938. (11)	Modern Age	.25
Vorse, M. H.	*Labor's New Millions.* 1937. (2)	Modern Age	.50
Wile, I. S.	*The Man Takes a Wife.* 1937. (5)	Greenberg	2.50
Wilson, Margery	*Your Personality and God.* 1938. (12)	Stokes	2.50
Wright, Milton	*The Art of Conversation.* 1936. (11)	Whittlesey	2.50

SCHEDULE OF MEETINGS

First Meeting: MY COUNTRY 'TIS OF THEE
1. Keeping the Peace
2. America and Americans

Second Meeting: SWEET LAND OF LIBERTY
1. Vigilance—Against What?
2. As the C.I.O. Sees It
3. A "Made in America" Radical

Third Meeting: THE MODERN WOMAN EMERGES
1. The American Woman's Background
2. Her Clubs and Her Politics
3. Sisters Under the Skin

Fourth Meeting: WOMEN AT WORK
1. Fields of Work for Women
2. Not Just a Job—But the Right Job
3. To Roam—or to Stay at Home?

Fifth Meeting: LIVING TOGETHER AND LIKING IT
1. The Long, Long History of Marriage
2. Turn About is Fair Play
3. For Women Only!
4. Marriage is What You Make It

Sixth Meeting: HOUSEKEEPING GOES MODERN
1. Imagination with Your Menus
2. More Value for Less Money
3. Housekeeping Without Tears

Seventh Meeting: PERPLEXED PARENTS
1. "But Why, Mother?"
2. "Excuse Us, We're in Our 'Teens!"
3. Guiding the 'Teen Age Girl

Eighth Meeting: YOUR CHILDREN FACE THEIR FUTURE
1. What Are the Problems of Youth?
2. Organizing the Community Survey

Ninth Meeting: WOMEN AND PUBLIC HEALTH
1. The People's Fight for Life
2. The Ghastly Luxury
3. Ills and Bills

Tenth Meeting: EVERYDAY HEALTH PROBLEMS
    1. What to Do—When
    2. Good Health and Grooming Day by Day
    3. Hearing is Believing

Eleventh Meeting: FIRST PERSON SINGULAR
    1. Trade Secrets of the Sex
    2. "A Good Time Was Had by All"
    3. You and Your Public

Twelfth Meeting: PURSUIT OF HAPPINESS
    1. On Enjoying Your Life
    2. And Reaping the Rewards of Enjoyment
    3. Every Day Begins a New Year

CPSIA information can be obtained
at www.ICGtesting.com
Printed in the USA
BVHW071010131218
535545BV00017B/884/P